Canada and the Global Village

Weigl Educational Publishers Limited

Published by Weigl Educational Publishers Limited
6325 – 10 Street SE
Calgary, Alberta, Canada
T2H 2Z9

Web site: www.weigl.com

All of the Internet URLs given in the book were valid at the time of publication.
However, due to the dynamic nature of the Internet, some addresses may have
changed, or sites may have ceased to exist since publication. While the author and
publisher regret any inconvenience this may cause readers, no responsibility for any
such changes can be accepted by either the author or the publisher.

Library and Archives Canada Cataloguing in Publication Data
Canada and the global village / Don Wells, editor.
(Canadian government)
Includes index.
ISBN 1-55388-068-4 (bound) ISBN 1-55388-123-0 (pbk)

1. Canada--Relations--Foreign countries--Textbooks. I. Wells, Don, 1953- II.
Series: Canadian government (Calgary, Alta.)
FC97.C278 2004   971   C2004-903627-0

Printed in the United States of America
1 2 3 4 5 6 7 8 9 0   09 08 07 06 05 04

We acknowledge the
financial support of the
Government of Canada
through the Book
Publishing Industry
Development Program
(BPIDP) for our
publishing activities.

Editor
Don Wells

Copy Editor
Heather Kissock

Photo Researcher
Ellen Byran

Designer
Warren Clark

Layout
Terry Paulhus

On the Cover
Canadian Forces soldiers
provide aid and supplies
to refugees in Kabul,
Afghanistan

Contents

Global Involvement

Canada promotes a global situation in which there is less chance for misunderstanding and conflict.

Following World War II, Lester B. Pearson wrote in his memoirs: "Everything I learned during the war confirmed and strengthened my view as a Canadian that our foreign policy must not be timid or fearful of commitments, but activist in accepting international responsibility." Pearson's attitude reflected that of many influential government leaders. Canada's postwar years thrust Canada into a level of participation in international and multilateral organizations that has continued to the present day.

Canadians have cooperated with both developed and developing countries to enhance world **security**, improve international communication, and reduce disparities in standards of living around the world. Through such interactions, Canada has reinforced its place as an influential global participant.

Canadarm

"Okay, the arm is out for the first time and it is working great. It's a remarkable flying machine and it's doing exactly as we hoped and expected."

In 1981, the Canadarm began its long service as an essential part of American space shuttles. The Canadarm is the first robotic manipulator system designed to be used in space. It has demonstrated its reliability, usefulness, and versatility on 63 space shuttle missions. The word "Canada" is displayed on the robotic manipulator's upper arm boom. The Canadarm is an important part of the U.S. space program. Canada already had a high reputation for developing technology for use in space before the creation of the Canadarm.

The Canadarm first travelled to space aboard the U.S. space shuttle Columbia.

Canada built the Alouette scientific satellite (1962), the CTS/Hermes experimental communications satellite (1976), the RADARSAT 1 Earth observation satellite (1995), and the Mobile Servicing System, which has a 17.2-metre long manipulator arm called Canadarm2 and was installed on the International Space Station in April 2001.

The Canadarm has been used to launch satellites into their proper orbit and retrieve satellites that need repair. Since December 1998, the arm has been used in 11 Space Station assembly missions. The Canadarm has been used to install new parts on the station and support spacewalks by space construction workers. It has been used to loosen a jammed solar array panel, and its elbow and wrist joint cameras have been used to visually inspect the orbiter and payload. It has also been used to knock ice off the shuttle's waste water dumping vents. The arm has been used by NASA for public relations activities. The Canadarm has two IMAX cameras attached to its lower boom. Many people have been able to enjoy the experience of space as a result of films made using the Canadarm.

Canadians are very fortunate. They have a land of numerous natural resources, a small population, a stable government, and a high standard of living. It can be easy to forget that others around the world live in desperate situations. Canadian policies have incorporated the idea that with privilege comes responsibility. Canada's relative wealth places it in a position to help many other nations deal with problems, such as overpopulation, climate change, famine, disease, war, and a scarcity of resources.

Multilateral and international institutions help deal with many of these problems. Canada belongs to organizations that have helped eliminate smallpox, addressed environmental degradation, and granted economic aid to struggling areas. By participating in such activities, Canada has shown its determination to be a good world citizen. Its actions have helped maintain stability and economic progress in many nations around the world.

Canada realizes that through communication comes knowledge, and through knowledge comes power. By actively participating in economic and political organizations, and by encouraging other nations to do the same, Canada promotes a global situation in which there is less chance for misunderstanding and conflicts. Through its participation and occasional leadership, Canada can keep a high international profile. This profile can, in turn, give Canada more global influence as it tries to persuade other nations to agree with policies of vital interest to Canada's own priorities. There are clearly almost as many reasons for being involved in international organizations as there are organizations themselves.

Canada spends billions dollars on **foreign aid**. Many argue that the Canadian government would be better off clearing up the country's deficit or creating jobs for its own people. Others suggest that Canadians do not have a choice. Global involvement is a necessary part of existing in the world community today. Many Canadians support global involvement through organizations like sports, **peacekeeping**, and foreign aid because they believe such involvements will help create a global community of cooperation rather than conflict.

Canadian troops have been stationed in many troubled countries as members of peacekeeping forces.

The Commonwealth of Nations

Canada belongs to many international organizations. These bodies do not have sovereign authority over members, but serve as forums for discussion and cooperation. Two of these organizations are directly linked to the two founding cultures of Canada.

When Britain's former colonies slowly gained their independence after 1931, they formed a free association to maintain friendship and cooperation. They called this association the Commonwealth of Nations. Due to their history as former British colonies, English is the common language for all nations. The British monarch is recognized as the symbolic head of the association.

The Commonwealth steadily grew from seven countries in 1931 to its current membership of fifty-one.

The heads of state meet every 2 years and sponsor such ventures as technical cooperation, scholarships, and the Commonwealth Games.

Canada played an important role in developing the organization. Canada's Prime Minister Lester Pearson was a key figure in negotiating a proposal that helped keep the former colonies linked to the Commonwealth. When India became independent in 1947, it wished to become a republic. This meant it did not want to recognize the Queen as its official head of government. Pearson proposed that the Queen remain the symbolic head of the Commonwealth, and that individual countries could choose whether to also place her as their head of government. This compromise allowed countries like India to form their own government, as well as retain Commonwealth status.

Canada has always encouraged the preservation of the association and has viewed it as a valuable diplomatic tool. The diplomatic contacts Canada makes through the Commonwealth help reduce its reliance on American foreign policy.

Like most long-standing institutions, the Commonwealth has undergone many changes. Some countries have left the Commonwealth because of conflicts with other members. Pakistan left because of differences with India in 1972, and South Africa left in 1961 when Commonwealth members pressured the country to abandon its apartheid policies. South Africa rejoined the Commonwealth on June 1, 1994 after beginning the process of dismantling apartheid.

The Commonwealth's strengths have always been cultural and developmental

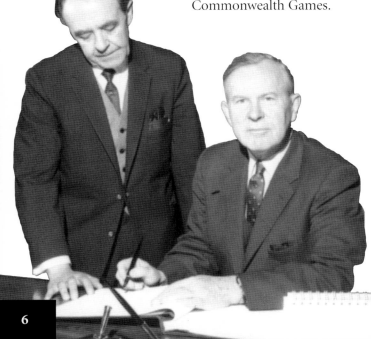

Lester B. Pearson became prime minister of Canada in 1963.

issues, while the organization tends to avoid highly charged political areas. Many leaders of Commonwealth nations fear that politically sensitive issues divide and drain the organization of resources. Commonwealth members discuss issues and try to reach a consensus on them, but they rarely call a vote, and their decisions are not legally binding on any member nation.

The Commonwealth is a unique group of nations with diverse religious, cultural, and racial backgrounds. Despite occasional conflicts, the Commonwealth stands as a positive example of international cooperation.

■ *A Commonwealth of Nations was proclaimed at the Imperial Conference of 1926.*

IN-DEPTH

Suspended Commonwealth Nations

The 1991 Harare Declaration is the most important statement of the Commonwealth's principles. The Harare Declaration states that the organization is dedicated to democracy and good government, human rights, gender equality, sustainable development, and environmental protection. It also establishes a process for

taking action against members who breach these principles. Before the Harare Declaration, the Commonwealth was limited by a policy of non-interference in the internal affairs of other members.

Since the Harare Declaration, the Commonwealth has suspended four countries

for not maintaining a democratic government. Suspended nations remain members of the organization, but they are not allowed to attend Commonwealth meetings. Fiji and Pakistan have been suspended from the organization for military coups. Fiji was suspended twice (1987–1997 and 2000–2001). Pakistan was suspended from 1999 until 2004. Nigeria was suspended in 1995 after executing

■ *The international community criticized the 2002 reelection of Robert Mugabe as president of Zimbabwe.*

activist and writer Ken Saro-Wiwa. Zimbabwe was suspended in 2002.

Membership in the Commonwealth is voluntary, and members can leave the organization at any time. Pakistan left in 1972 because the Commonwealth recognized Bangladesh, which had been part of Pakistan. Pakistan rejoined the Commonwealth in 1989. Zimbabwe left in 2003 when the Commonwealth refused to lift the country's suspension. The Commonwealth was still concerned about Zimbabwe's record on human rights and the apparent lack of democratic government in the country.

International Organization

The G8 chair rotates each year among the seven original member nations.

La Francophonie has many similarities to the Commonwealth. Both organizations are formed from countries that share a colonial history, and both work toward similar goals of international cooperation. La Francophonie, however, is linked by French as a common language, not English.

The organization began in 1967 in Luxembourg, and it fosters cooperation and development aid among member states in areas such as culture, science, and education. Unlike organizations such as the Commonwealth, however, there are no regular summit meetings.

Not all of Canada's memberships are in cultural organizations. One of the most influential organizations Canada belongs to is concerned almost solely with economic matters.

The Group of Eight, or G8 as it is more commonly known, links the world's largest economies. The G8 was the brainchild of finance ministers from France and Germany in the early 1970s. The ministers wanted the most industrialized nations in the world to join forces against the Organization of Petroleum Exporting Countries (OPEC) oil cartel. In 1975, France, the United States, Britain, Germany, Japan, and Italy met to discuss economic and political issues of concern to their countries and the international community. Canada joined in 1976. Russia joined in 1998. The G8 also includes the European Union. Membership in the G8 depends, at least in theory, upon being one of the largest eight economies in the world.

The primary aim of the organization has been to encourage members to exchange information regarding their economic policies. The G8 has played a leadership role on issues of trade and finance and has created policies to

SOMMET D'EVIAN
2003

1-2-3 JUIN

help improve the global economy. Within the last few years, the G8 has also addressed issues such as job creation, environmental pollution, and global communication.

Canada has hosted four summits since 1976: Ottawa-Montebello, 1981; Toronto, 1988; Halifax, 1995; and Kananaskis, Alberta, 2002.

Canada's membership in the G8 enables the country to pursue its broad foreign and economic policies and interests, help shape global developments, and respond to global crises.

IN-DEPTH

North Atlantic Treaty Organization (NATO)

In response to the **Cold War**, the nations of western Europe, the United States, and Canada moved to protect their interests and prevent the spread of communism. They formed the North Atlantic **Treaty** Organization (NATO) on April 4, 1949. NATO provided for collective defence among member countries and arranged for improved international relations through discussions on human rights, **arms control**, **trade**, and other issues. Through the alliance, nations would cooperate in non-military matters such as assisting developing nations, scientific research, and environmental protection.

While the United States and Canada were reluctant to support the idea of collective security after World War II, they now fully embraced the idea. This change was at least partially due to the design of weapons that put their own territories at risk.

Besides NATO's security benefits, many Canadians

■ *NATO is also involved in peacekeeping missions.*

supported NATO involvement because it promoted increased economic ties to Europe and its markets.

NATO is governed by the North Atlantic Council. NATO members hold ongoing military talks, coordinate defence planning, and run joint military exercises. They also maintain a number of troops in order to provide for their common defence.

NATO had several strategies with which to halt a Soviet attack. The first goal was to stop a Soviet invasion as far east as possible. This would protect Western Europe from the destruction it would incur as a battleground.

NATO also adopted the strategy of flexible response. In the event of an attack, NATO forces would be prepared to fight in a variety of ways. Beginning with conventional weapons, NATO would escalate the conflict, if necessary, to small, tactical nuclear weapons, and would resort to full-scale nuclear war as a last resort.

In 1969, Canada reduced its commitment to NATO and froze military spending. The three main reasons given for this action were the high cost of weapons, the tendency of the superpowers to discuss differences without consulting Canada, and the growing tension between China and the Soviet Union, which reduced the threat to Europe. The NATO force was cut from about 100,000 to 78,000.

In 1992, the government announced that, by 1995, Canadian Forces Europe would cease to exist. Canadian Forces Europe provided the basis of Canada's NATO commitment for more than 40 years. This withdrawal was due to lessening Cold War tensions and a wish to use Canadian troops to maintain Canadian peacekeeping duties.

Canada's financial contribution to NATO was $140 Million in 2003. In 2004, Canada was involved in NATO-led peacekeeping operations in Afghanistan and Bosnia-Herzegovina.

International Sports

The Olympic flag, which shows the five Olympic rings, first flew at the 1920 Olympic Games in Antwerp, Belgium.

While Canada participates in the serious economic and political arenas, there is another, more casual international arena in which Canada participates: sporting events. International sports serve many purposes. They foster cross-cultural understanding while putting each individual on a level playing field, no matter where they are from. They give countries and their citizens a sense of identity and pride while celebrating the spirit of competition.

The Olympics are the most celebrated sporting event of all. The modern version of the games was organized in 1896 to encourage world peace and friendship, as well as to promote amateur athletics and revive the Olympic values of harmonizing physical, mental, and spiritual development. The first modern games were held in Athens,

and they have been held every 4 years since, except during World Wars I and World War II. Although there were Canadian participants in some of the early events, Canada sent its first official national team of eighty-four athletes to London in 1908.

The Olympic symbol of five interlocking rings is a story in **internationalism** itself. Each ring represents the continents of Africa, Asia, Australia, Europe, and North and South America. Even the colours of black, blue, green, red, and yellow hold significance. Every nation competing in the Olympics includes at least one of those colours on its flag.

Canada has hosted the Olympics twice: the 1976 Summer Olympics in Montréal and the 1988 Winter Olympics in Calgary. Host cities incur large expenses to ensure their city and sporting facilities are showcases for

their country. Through hosting an event like the Olympics, host countries gain world recognition and status.

Despite their lofty mandate and ideals, the Olympic Games have seen controversy and politics. In 1980, Canada was one of many countries to **boycott** the Moscow Summer Games as a protest against the Soviet Union's invasion of Afghanistan. The boycott was a diplomatic tool used to voice concern about the Soviet Union's military aggression.

Many of the athletes were angered that government policy could rob them of their opportunity to compete against the world's finest athletes. Athletes train very hard for years to gain the chance to enter Olympic competition. For some, the 1980 Olympics was their only chance.

The Commonwealth Games, although smaller in stature and only for those athletes from Commonwealth countries, are similar to the Olympic Games in their objectives. The original intent was to "draw closer the ties between nations of the Empire." The first official games were held in 1930 in Hamilton, Ontario. Like the Olympics, they have been held every 4 years since then, except during the two World Wars.

Some view the Commonwealth Games as preparation for the Olympics. Canadian athletes such as swimmer Alex Baumann perfected their crafts through Commonwealth competition. These games differ from the Olympics in that they distinguish between a country and a nation. While there is no official United Kingdom team competing at the Commonwealth Games, there are teams from the four nations of England, Scotland, Wales, and Northern Ireland.

DOCUMENT

The 1980 Olympics

The Canadian Olympic Association passed a resolution that explained its boycott of the 1980 Moscow Summer Games.

AFTER DUE DELIBERATION the Canadian Olympic Association hereby RESOLVES

THAT it deeply regrets the international situation which now exists as a result of the invasion of Afghanistan by armed forces of the Soviet Union;

THAT it joins the International Olympic Committee in calling upon the governments of all countries, and in particular those of the major powers, to come together to resolve their differences so that the Games of the XXII Olympiad can take place in the right atmosphere;

THAT it completely rejects the proposition that either the awarding of the Games of the XXII Olympiad to Moscow or participation in such Games is in any way a vindication of the foreign policy of the Soviet Union;

THAT because of the current international situation it would not be appropriate for Canadian athletes to participate in the Games of the XXII Olympiad and that in this regard the Canadian Olympic Association takes note of the advice of the Government of Canada that participation would be contrary to the national interest;

■ *More than 60 nations boycotted the 1980 Olympic Summer Games in Moscow.*

THAT accordingly the Canadian Olympic Association will not accept the invitation to participate in the Games of the XXII Olympiad;

THAT the Canadian Olympic Association reserves the right to reassess the present decision in light of a change in circumstances which might indicate that it would become appropriate to participate in the Games of the XXII Olympiad;

THAT, notwithstanding any final decision not to participate, the Canadian Olympic Association will select and honour the athletes who comprise the Canadian team for the Games of the XXII Olympiad to recognize their commitment to excellence in sport and the sacrifice which has been thrust upon them by any decision not to compete in the Games.

The United Nations

Representatives from Canada helped create the United Nations Charter.

While sporting events and regular meetings may alleviate some conflicts, they have not succeeded in eliminating armed clashes. After the devastation of World War II, many countries decided to band together formally to try to prevent and resolve conflict before it escalated to a third world war.

On October 24, 1945, fifty countries created the United Nations (UN) with internationalism as its founding principle. Canada was one of the original nations to sign the United Nations Charter.

By 2002, the United Nations had grown to 191 countries. In recent years, debates in the United Nations have included nuclear power and disarmament, the use of outer space, the status of women and children, terrorism, human rights, world hunger, and the destruction of the environment.

The United Nations has four main purposes. The first is to maintain international peace and security. Its members have agreed to take collective action to prevent and remove threats and to suppress acts of aggression. Canada argued that the United Nations should create its own army using soldiers and money from all the member countries.

Members were reluctant to take this step, so they agreed to donate troops and equipment from their own forces when required. This gave them the option of accepting or refusing to participate in individual conflicts. All agreed to use peaceful means, whenever possible, for the settlement of international disputes.

The second purpose of the United Nations is to develop friendly relations among nations based on respect for the equal rights and self-determination of all peoples.

HAITI   CANADA   REECE   ...RABIA   HONDURAS

The third purpose is to achieve international cooperation in solving problems of an economic, social, cultural, or humanitarian nature. The members have agreed to promote and encourage respect for human rights without distinction as to race, sex, language, or religion.

The final purpose is to serve as a centre for coordinating the actions of nations in attempting to achieve the purposes of the United Nations. Continued support of the United Nations is a basic element of Canadian foreign policy.

Thousands of people are influenced directly or indirectly by the United Nations. Each day, in some part of the world, United Nations employees or volunteers work to bring a better standard of living to people. The United Nations fights poverty, hunger, disease, unemployment, and illiteracy. As part of this policy, the United Nations also supports measures to ensure world peace.

IN-DEPTH

United Nations Rules on Québec Sign Law

Gordon McIntyre, a businessperson in Québec, took his opposition to Bill 178, also known as the sign law, to the United Nations. Bill 178 requires all commercial signs in Québec to be in French. McIntyre had a sign in English only, and he refused to take this sign down without a fight. McIntyre complained to the United Nations Human Rights Committee in 1989, after an official from the Office de la Langue Français told him to remove the English outdoor sign on his Huntingdon funeral home in accordance with Québec's French-only sign law.

In 1993, the eighteen people who serve on the UN Human Rights Committee in Geneva, Switzerland, ruled that Bill 178 violated the international standards of freedom of expression.

The UN's Human Rights Committee ruled that Canada had violated part of Article 19 of the International Convenant on Civil and Political Rights, which states that everyone has the right to freedom of expression.

The decision carries no legal weight, even though Canada has signed the human rights covenant. However, as a result of the ruling, Québec changed its French-only sign law. Highway billboards and public transport signs are still restricted to French, but businesses can post signs in English as long as the sign is also written in French and the French lettering is twice as large as the English lettering.

■ *In 1988, the Supreme Court of Canada ruled that Québec could legally require "greater visibility" or "marked prominence" of French on signs.*

Structure of the United Nations

The UN General Assembly is composed of all the member countries. Its members meet annually at UN headquarters in New York City. The General Assembly does not enact laws. Instead, it makes recommendations on subjects that are within the scope of its charter. The General Assembly has been called the "town meeting of the world." Each member country may have as many as five delegates but only one vote.

The General Assembly calls attention to international problems and is empowered to discuss and make recommendations regarding them. The decisions of the General Assembly are not binding on any nation. They are only expressions of world opinion.

The General Assembly also appoints the secretary-general of the United Nations and directs the work of the Secretariat. It elects the non-permanent members of the Security Council, and together with the Security Council, it elects the judges of the World Court. It also receives and discusses reports from all other branches of the United Nations.

Security Council

The Charter of the United Nations gives the Security Council the authority to settle international disputes through peaceful means. If peaceful means do not work, then the Security Council can use whatever means necessary to maintain peace. The Council meets in continuous session, and its members are on call 24 hours a day.

The Security Council is made up of fifteen members, including five permanent members—the United States, the Russian Federation, Great Britain, the People's Republic of China, and France. The other members are elected for 2-year terms.

The Security Council has considerable power. If world peace is threatened, the Security Council may

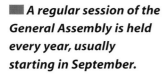
A regular session of the General Assembly is held every year, usually starting in September.

request that members of the United Nations stop relations with the parties in dispute. It may also order sanctions that all United Nations' members are supposed to follow.

If the Security Council decides to take military action, it must have the approval of all five permanent members and a majority vote of the other members. Each of the permanent members has the right of veto. If even one of them votes against a course of action, then the action cannot be taken.

Secretariat

The Secretariat has full responsibility for the administration of the United Nations. In 2001, this worldwide organization had over 15,000 employees. The Secretariat is headed by the secretary-general. The secretary-general may call the attention of the Security Council to any situation that may pose a threat to world peace and security.

Economic and Social Council

The Economic and Social Council meets twice a year. Its aim is the prevention of war through the adjustment of economic and social problems. It is concerned with improving economic, social, cultural, educational, and health conditions around the world.

The Economic and Social Council's commissions and committees deal with human rights, the control of narcotics, crime, and the status of women.

International Court of Justice

The International Court of Justice deals with international legal problems. It is located at The Hague in the Netherlands. The World Court, as it is sometimes called, is composed of fifteen judges elected by the General Assembly and the Security Council for 9-year terms. These judges represent the principal legal systems of the world. The Court hears cases brought before it by member states. It also interprets the terms of treaties and international law.

DOCUMENT

The Charter of the United Nations (excerpt)

WE THE PEOPLES OF THE UNITED NATIONS DETERMINED to save succeeding generations from the scourge of war, which twice in our lifetime has brought untold sorrow to mankind, and to reaffirm our faith in fundamental human rights, in the dignity and worth of the human person, in the equal rights of men and women and of nations large and small, and to establish conditions under which justice and respect for the obligations arising from treaties and other sources of international law can be maintained, and to promote social progress and better standards of life in larger freedom.

AND FOR THESE ENDS to practice tolerance and live together in peace with one another as good neighbours, and to unite our strength to maintain international peace and security, and to ensure, by the acceptance of principles and the institution of methods, that armed force shall not be used, save in the common interest, and to employ international machinery for the promotion of the economic and social advancement of all peoples,

HAVE RESOLVED TO COMBINE OUR EFFORTS TO ACCOMPLISH THESE AIMS. Accordingly, our respective governments, through representatives assembled in the city of San Francisco, who have exhibited their full powers found to be in good and due form, have agreed to the present Charter of the United Nations and do hereby establish an international organization to be known as the United Nations.

PROVISIONS FOR AMENDMENT
Any alteration of the Charter recommended by a two-thirds vote of the members of the General Assembly shall take effect when ratified by two-thirds of the members of the United Nations" in accordance with their respective constitutional processes" including all the permanent members of the Security Council.

Peacekeeping

The purpose of peacekeeping is not only to halt conflict, but also to create the conditions in which the search for peaceful solutions can take place through negotiations.

A continuing feature of Canada's foreign policy has been an overall commitment to promote international peace and security. The participation of Canadian troops in United Nations'

peacekeeping missions and related operations has helped eased tensions in trouble spots around the world.

As a responsible member of the international community, Canada seeks

■ *Canadian troops represent Canada in many international events and missions. Every year since 1952, Canadian troops have participated in the Nijmegen Marches held in the Netherlands.*

IN-DEPTH

Scandal in Somalia

In 1992, the United Nations sent peacekeepers to help distribute **humanitarian aid** to starving people in war-torn Somalia. The actions of some Canadian soldiers in Somalia tarnished the reputation of Canadian peacekeepers.

About 900 members of the Canadian Airborne Regiment arrived in Somalia in 1992. Soldiers on patrol shot two Somalis on March 4, 1993. One of these people was wounded, and the other died. Twelve days later, a teenaged

Somali was tortured and killed on the UN base in Belet Huen, located near Somalia's border with Ethiopia. A Canadian soldier took photographs of the torturous acts. These images, along with videotape of the conduct of these

soldiers became public. The regiment was disbanded, and its actions were investigated. Many officers lost their jobs, and some soldiers were tried and sent to prison for their actions.

Peacekeeping in places such as Somalia is an important part of Canada's national heritage, and it reflects the fundamental beliefs of Canadians.

the maintenance of a peaceful international order. Peace is the best condition in which Canada can pursue its own interests. Canadian troops contribute to this international order through peacekeeping operations, arms control verification, and humanitarian assistance.

Canadian troops have always been at the forefront of United Nations' efforts to keep peace. Canada has sent troops and observers to such distant places as Kashmir, West New Guinea, and Yemen.

The United Nations stresses two main forms of peacekeeping. Observers are sent to supervise a truce, or armed forces are sent to keep peace between combatants. UN peacekeeping operations use the troops of neutral countries to separate opposing sides. These troops try to resolve further disagreements and stop armed conflict from erupting again. The UN sends troops only when disputing countries agree to their presence.

Canada recognizes that international peacekeeping has many limitations and should not be viewed as an end in itself. The purpose of peacekeeping is not only to halt conflict, but also to create the conditions in which the search for peaceful solutions can take place through negotiations.

Canada has also participated in peacekeeping missions not sponsored by the United Nations. Canada sent an International Observer Team to Nigeria in 1968–1969. Canadian forces were also involved in two truce supervisory operations in Indochina and have been part of the Multinational Force and Observers in the Sinai since 1986. As well, between 1991 and 1994, Canada was part of the **European Community** Monitor Mission in the former Yugoslav republics.

FURTHER UNDERSTANDING

Royal Canadian Mounted Police (RCMP) and Peacekeeping

The main objective of the RCMP's Civilian Police Peacekeeping Operations is to manage Canadian civilian police participating in international peacekeeping activities. These services are provided as part of Canada's foreign policy requirements. They are funded by the Canadian International Development Agency (CIDA), the Department of Foreign Affairs and International Trade (DFAIT), Public Safety and Emergency Preparedness Canada, and the RCMP. Provincial and municipal police forces also contribute personnel to various peacekeeping missions.

Canada in Korea

■ *Canadians accepted American leadership in opposition to communist expansion in Korea. However, Prime Minister Pearson emphasized that Canada's participation was part of a United Nations operation, not an American one.*

After the defeat of the Japanese in World War II, the United States and the Soviet Union occupied Korea. The country was divided at the 38th Parallel, with the Americans controlling the South and the Soviets controlling the North. The original aim was to reunite the country, but as relations between the United States and the Soviet Union worsened, unification attempts stopped.

In 1947, the Americans asked the United Nations General Assembly to call for the evacuation of all occupying forces from Korea. The United States wanted North Korea and South Korea to hold free elections. A United Nations Commission was established to ensure the plan was carried out. However, the Soviets refused to accept the United Nations plan, and the commission was forced to confine its efforts to South Korea.

Free elections were held in the South and a pro-American government was elected. In the North, the Soviets helped establish a communist government.

In June 1950, North Korea invaded South Korea. This was an important event for the United Nations because it was the first time since its inception that a member nation had been invaded by another country.

At a meeting of the United Nations Security Council on the Korean invasion, the United States called on the North Koreans to end the fighting and withdraw. The Soviet delegate to the Security Council was boycotting the session at the time because of Cold War differences with the United Sates. The Soviet absence meant the United States was able to push its motion through the Security Council.

When North Korea ignored the United Nations call to withdraw, the

United Nations sent a military force to protect South Korea. This force included troops from the United States, Canada, the Union of South Africa, Australia, New Zealand, Turkey, Belgium, the Netherlands, and Great Britain. The decision to send troops at this point in the conflict was important because it showed that the United Nations was willing to use force to impose its will. This willingness to take action marked the UN as different from the League of Nations, which had proven incapable of stopping aggression.

During the Korean conflict, Canadian Forces fought under the United Nations banner. Canada was careful to insist that it participated as part of the United Nations force, and not as part of the American forces.

Approximately 27,000 members of the Royal Canadian Navy, Canadian Army, and Royal Canadian Air Force served in the Korean War over a span of 3 years. The Canadians suffered more than 1,600 casualties, including 516 deaths.

Canadian participation in the United Nations Command Military Armistice Commission began in 1953 with the conclusion of the Korean War. Until 2000, the Canadian Forces Attaché in Seoul was a member of the Military Armistice Commission for 6 months every 2 years. This Commission was charged with supervising the implementation of the 1953 Armistice Agreement to settle negotiations of violations of the Agreement and act as intermediary between commanders of the opposing sides.

ACTIVE CITIZENSHIP

Tommy Prince

Tommy Prince is Canada's most-decorated Aboriginal war veteran. He was a member of a specialized 1600-man assault team. This team became the 1st Special Service Force, known as the "Devil's Brigade."

In Italy, Prince ran a 1,400-metre communications line to an abandoned farmhouse less than 200 metres from a German camp. Artillery shells cut the wire. Prince disguised himself as a farmer and found and repaired the wire as German soldiers watched him. For his actions, he was awarded the Military Medal for "exceptional bravery in the field."

In the summer of 1944, Prince walked 70 kilometres across mountains behind German lines near L'Escarene, France. He went 72 hours without food or water and located an enemy camp. He led his unit to the camp, where they captured more than 1,000 German soldiers. He earned the Silver Star, an American decoration for gallantry in action, as well as six service medals during World War II.

When Prince returned to Canada after the end of World War II, he, along with all Aboriginal Peoples, was not allowed to vote in federal elections, and he did not receive the same benefits as other Canadian veterans.

When the Korean War started, Prince enlisted in the Princess Patricia's Canadian Light Infantry. During two tours of duty in the

> "All my life I had wanted to do something to help my people recover their good name."

Korean War, his unit won the United States' Presidential Unit Citation for distinguished service. Prince also received the Korea Medal and the United Nations Service Medal. He was wounded in the knee and was honourably discharged on October 28, 1953.

Prince felt it was his duty to fight for his country, and he was very proud of his heritage. He said, "All my life I had wanted to do something to help my people recover their good name. I wanted to show they were as good as any white man." After the Korean War, Prince worked to obtain increased educational and economic opportunities for Aboriginal Peoples.

Canada in the Middle East

Canada has been active in Middle East peacekeeping missions since 1954.

■ *In 1964, Canadian peacekeepers helped patrol the Sinai desert in the region between Israel and Palestine.*

While Korea marked the first United Nations military involvement, the Middle East was the site of the first United Nations peacekeeping effort.

During World War II, over six million Jewish people were killed in concentration camps. After the war, the horrors of the camps caused worldwide shock and concern. Many people supported the establishment of a national Jewish homeland in the hope that this would prevent future persecution of Jews.

Although Jews had been scattered throughout Europe and Asia since the sixth century BC, Palestine was considered the traditional homeland of the Jews. Following the two world wars, large numbers of displaced Jews moved to Palestine. The number of Jews in the country grew from 84,000 in 1922 to 625,000 in 1947.

Although the British had occupied Palestine since World War I, Arabs viewed this increased Jewish immigration as a threat to the country they had lived in for generations. Both Arabs and Jews began terrorist activities against one another and against the British occupation force. As the British lost hope that they could control the growing tensions, they passed the problem to the United Nations and announced a date for their withdrawal.

The United Nations tried to solve the problem by dividing Palestine into separate Arab and Jewish states, creating Israel as the Jewish homeland in 1948. The creation of Israel angered the surrounding Arab states, so they attacked the new nation. However, instead of destroying Israel, the Arabs were defeated, with Israel gaining control of even more land. As conflicts continued over the next 2 decades, Israel continued its military success by winning several strategically important pieces of land: the Golan Heights, the Gaza Strip, and the West Bank.

For decades, conflict has been a permanent fixture of the area. The Israelis have tried to create a buffer zone around Israel to protect the country from Arab attack. The Arabs have not recognized the state of Israel, and some still want to destroy it.

A United Nations Truce Supervision Organization was established in 1949 to observe and maintain cease-fires in the disputed territories. Canada has been active in Middle East peacekeeping missions since 1954. Canada currently contributes military observers, liaison officers, and headquarter staff. This operation has a mandate of indefinite duration.

IN-DEPTH

Peacekeeping Missions

Since the earliest days of peacekeeping, Canadian peacekeepers have been involved in the Middle East. In 2003, Canada was involved in three peacekeeping missions in the region.

Operation CALUMET

Operation CALUMET is the name of Canada's contribution to the Multinational Force and Observers (MFO) mission. MFO's mission is to observe and report on adherence to the Camp David Accords. The Accords is a three-way agreement between Egypt, Israel, and the United States signed in 1979. With this agreement, which was denounced by other Arab states, Israel agreed to return the Sinai to Egypt. This transfer was completed in 1982. In a joint letter, Egypt and Israel also agreed to negotiate Palestinian autonomy in the Israeli-occupied West Bank and Gaza Strip. The issue of Palestinian autonomy is still a serious point of conflict between Israel and Palestinians. Canada has participated in the MFO mission since March 1986. Twenty-nine Canadian Forces personnel were assigned to this mission in 2003. They included staff officers, air traffic controllers, and administrative support personnel. The Canadian peacekeepers were based at El Gorah, Egypt. The mission has a continuing mandate.

Operation DANACA

Operation DANACA is the name of Canada's contribution to the United Nations Disengagement Observer Force, or UNDOF, in the Golan Heights region, which straddles the border between Israel and Syria. This mission began in 1974 to supervise the cease-fire between Israel and Syria. In 2003, 193 Canadian Forces personnel

■ *Peacekeepers observe the actions of those involved in the conflict in the Golan Heights from UN observation posts.*

were attached to UNDOF. They include supply, maintenance, and communications specialists. The United Nations Security Council reviews the mandate of this mission every 6 months.

Operation JADE

Operation JADE is the name of Canada's contribution to the United Nations Truce Supervisory Organization, or UNTSO. In 1948, the United Nations formed UNTSO to observe and maintain the cease-fire between Israel, Egypt, Lebanon, Jordan, and Syria. There are eight Canadian Forces officers who work as United Nations Military Observers. In 2003, there were Canadian observers on the Golan Heights, in South Lebanon, and in the Sinai to monitor cease-fire agreements, supervise troop movements, and observe events in contested areas. The mission began in 1954, and it has an indefinite duration. Operation JADE is Canada's longest-running peacekeeping mission.

Suez Canal

In 1952, events in the Middle East seemed to point the world in the direction of another war. Egypt, under President Nasser, was determined to build a new dam to irrigate vast portions of the desert and supply power for industry.

The Aswan Dam was a huge project, and Egypt sought loans from the United States and Great Britain to pay for it. However, the West was uneasy about Egypt's friendly relations with the Soviet Union, and in July, 1956, they refused the Aswan Dam loan. Shortly afterwards, Egypt took control of the internationally owned Suez Canal, announcing it would use the canal tolls to pay for the Aswan Dam. Great Britain and France, each with vested interests in the Canal, demanded that Egypt withdraw and the canal be placed under international control.

Great Britain and France, with Israel's help, attacked Egypt on October 29, 1956. Great Britain and France defended their participation by stating that they were ensuring free international passage through the canal. In retaliation, Egypt blocked the Suez Canal by sinking forty ships.

The Suez Canal

Bursa ·   ★ Ankara   zey Anadolu Dağı   ★ Yerevan   AZERBAIJAN   ★ Baku

Lesbos ·   Izmir ·   T U R K E Y   Sivas ·   Erzincan ·   Kara'köse ·   Archivah ·

Afyon ·   Kayseri ·   Tabriz ·   Ardabil

Mugla ·   Konya ·   Elazig ·   Lahijan ·   Babol Sar ·

Antalya ·   · Adana   Urfa ·   Mosel ·   Zanjan ·   Elbourz Mounta

Rhodes ·   · Aleppo   Kirkuk ·

Iraklion ·   **Nicosia**   SYRIA   Hamadan ·   **Tehran**

Crete ·   ★   Al Mayadin ·   Bakhtaran ·

CYPRUS   **Beirut**   **Damascus**   Arak ·

M e d i t e r r a n e a n   S e a   LEBANON ★   ★   **Baghdad** ★   Esfahan ·

The Suez Canal   **Tel Aviv**   IRAQ   Zagros Mountains

Alexandria ·   ISRAEL ★   ★ **Amman**   Andimeshk ·   Abadeh ·

Port Said ·   Turayf ·   As Samawah ·

Qattara Depression   Suez ·   JORDAN   Basra ·   Shiraz ·

Cairo ★   Sinai Pen.   ★ **Kuwait**   Helleylah ·

Beni Suef ·   S A U D I   A R A B I A   KUWAIT

El-Minya ·   Tabuk ·   Hafar Al Batin ·

Tayma ·   *Persian Gulf*

N   Buraydah ·   **Al Manamah** ★

· Qena   Al Majmaah ·   BAHRAIN

E G Y P T   **Ad Dawha**

0   250   500 km   Medina ·   ★ **Riyadh**   ★ QATAR   Abu Dhabi

· Aswan   Al Hilwah ·   U.A.

Red Sea

When fighting began in late October, the United Nations was unable to cope immediately with the crisis. At an emergency meeting of the General Assembly to consider a cease-fire resolution, Lester B. Pearson, Canada's foreign minister, recommended that the United Nations establish an international police force to keep the borders at peace until a settlement could be worked out. His suggestion was approved by the General Assembly. For his work, Lester Pearson was awarded the Nobel Peace Prize in 1957.

The General Assembly resolution established the first peacekeeping force, as distinct from observer groups already deployed in many countries by the United Nations. A cease-fire was finally arranged, and a peacekeeping force was sent to the Suez. A Canadian major-general was appointed to head this United Nations Emergency Force (UNEF).

The Egyptians objected to Canadian forces in the United Nations troops. They believed the Canadian army was too associated with Britain to be an impartial participant. Canada altered its peacekeeping commitment by sending service and supply troops instead of infantry.

In 1967, Egypt demanded the removal of all United Nations troops from its territories. United Nations Secretary-General U Thant agreed because the United Nations peacekeeping mandate insists that it must have consent to remain in a country.

War broke out almost immediately after the United Nations withdrew. Israel attacked Egypt, trying to pre-empt an attack. Other Arab nations joined Egypt in retaliation, and the United Nations again sent in a peacekeeping force.

Canada continues to participate in peacekeeping operations in the Middle East. Approximately 572 regular and reserve force members provide logistics, communications, and technical support to the United Nations force.

PROFILE

Lester Bowles Pearson

One of the few diplomats to ever receive international recognition, Lester B. (Mike) Pearson was the recipient of the 1957 Nobel Peace Prize for creating the first United Nations Peacekeeping Force. The force he proposed is often credited with preventing another world war over the Suez Crisis. At the time, he was Minister of External Affairs for Canada.

Born in 1897, Pearson was educated at the University of Toronto and Oxford. Later, he taught history at the University of Toronto. Finding a professor's salary difficult to live on, Pearson joined the Department of External Affairs and rose quickly through the ranks. From 1935 to 1941, he was attached to the Canadian High Commission in London, England.

Pearson served as Minister of External Affairs from 1948 to 1957, and oversaw Canada's involvement in the Korean War, as well as the creation of the North Atlantic Treaty Organization (NATO). Throughout his career, he maintained a strong interest in the United Nations.

In April 1963, Pearson became Canada's fourteenth prime minister,

■ *Lester B. Pearson was the first Canadian to receive a Nobel Peace Prize.*

heading a minority government. He called another election in 1965, hoping to secure a majority, but again won only a minority government.

His considerable legacy to Canada includes the Canadian flag, the Canada Pension Plan, universal medicare, and the unified Canadian Armed Forces.

Canada in Cyprus

In 1964, troops from Canada, Finland, Denmark, Ireland, and Sweden arrived in Cyprus.

◼ Canadian soldiers worked with the UN peacekeeping force in Cyprus to maintain law and order.

Canadians were proud of their role in the creation of the first peacekeeping force. This pride lent support to more peacekeeping involvements. One of Canada's longest peacekeeping missions was in Cyprus.

The island of Cyprus left British control and became an independent sovereign republic in 1959. Since the majority of Cypriots were Greek, negotiators agreed that the president of Cyprus would always be a Greek Cypriot. Cyprus also had a Turkish minority, so they agreed that the vice-president would be a Turkish Cypriot.

Unfortunately, the Greek and Turkish Cypriots were unable to co-operate, and fighting broke out between the two groups in 1963. When both Greece and Turkey threatened to intervene to support their respective peoples, Cyprus agreed to allow British troops to return and restore order.

In February 1964, Britain appealed to the United Nations Security Council for help. The United Nations agreed to station forces between the two ethnic groups. In March 1964, troops from Canada, Finland, Denmark, Ireland, and Sweden arrived in Cyprus.

In 1974, Turkey invaded Cyprus because it feared the Greek Cypriots were planning to take over the island. The United Nations sent in more troops to prevent continued fighting between Greek and Turkish Cypriots, as well as between the Cypriot National Guard and Turkey's armed forces.

As a result of the fighting, the island was forcibly partitioned in 1975. An area under Turkish control was established in the northern part of the island. The remainder of the island was placed under Greek Cypriot control. This partition led to a United Nations sponsored agreement in 1978 to permanently divide the island into two republics.

In December 1992, the Canadian government notified the United Nations that it would withdraw its contingent in 1993. Canada did agree, however, to retain a small number of personnel in Cyprus.

IN-DEPTH

A New Type of Peacekeeping

Within 24 hours of invading Cyprus, Turkish troops were poised to capture the airport on the western end of the city of Nicosia. UN commanders decided that allowing the Turkish troops to capture the airport would be a blow to UN credibility.

The airport was declared a UN protected zone. Canada's UNFICYP (United Nations Peacekeeping Force in Cyprus) contingent was sent to protect the airport. The first assault by Turkish troops was repelled by Greek Cypriot defences. When the Turkish troops prepared for a second assault, the Canadian peacekeepers reminded both sides that they had agreed to a cease-fire. The Canadian soldiers told the Turkish troops Canadian troops would defend the airport. The Turkish commanders were also told that any attack would result in bad press for Turkey, which would be condemned for attacking UN peacekeeping troops.

The Turkish troops could have easily overrun the Canadian positions, but they decided not to attack. They were sure the Canadians would hold their ground.

The Canadian troops successfully defended the airport and ushered in a new type of peacekeeping. Instead of passively occupying the ground between two opposing forces, the Canadian forces actively intervened between the two opposing sides.

■ *The Nicosia airport in Cyprus is still controlled by the United Nations.*

Mapping the Commonwealth of Nations

The citizens of Commonwealth nations make up 30 percent of the world's population: India is the most populous member, with one billion people at the 2001 census, while Pakistan, Bangladesh, and Nigeria each contain more than 100 million people. Tuvalu, by contrast, has only 11,000 inhabitants.

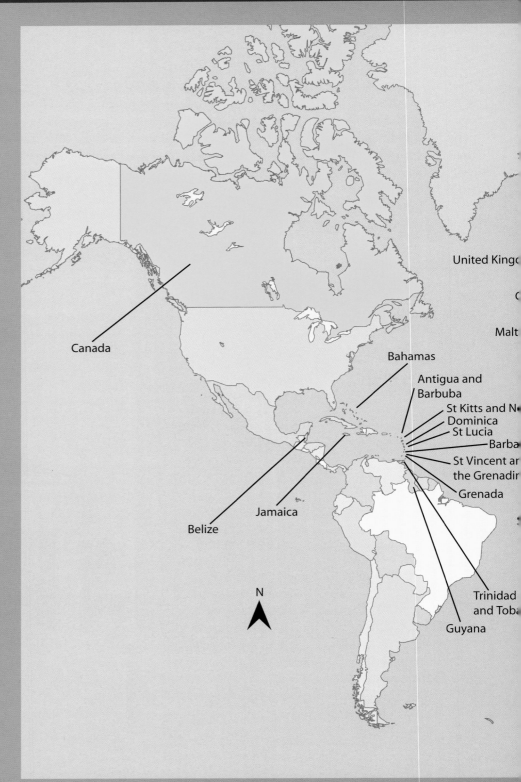

Canada

United Kingo

Malt

Bahamas

Antigua and Barbuba

St Kitts and N

Dominica

St Lucia

Barba

St Vincent ar the Grenadir

Grenada

Jamaica

Belize

N

Trinidad and Toba

Guyana

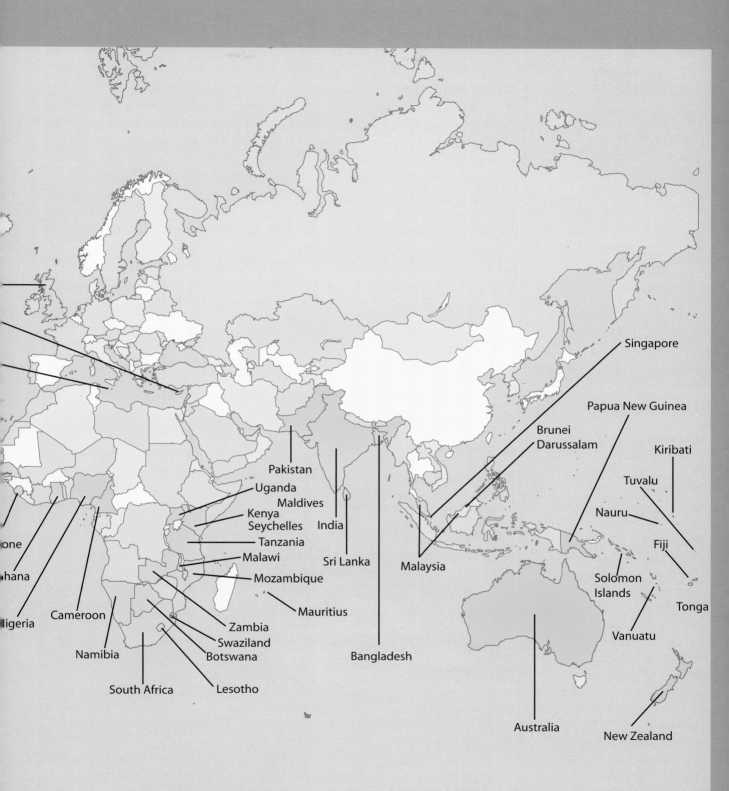

Singapore

Papua New Guinea

Brunei
Darussalam

Kiribati

Pakistan

Tuvalu

Uganda
Maldives
Kenya
Seychelles

Nauru

India

Tanzania

Fiji

Malawi

Sri Lanka

Mozambique

Malaysia

Mauritius

Solomon
Islands

Tonga

one

Zambia

hana

Swaziland

Vanuatu

Cameroon

Botswana

igeria

Namibia

Bangladesh

South Africa

Lesotho

Australia

New Zealand

Canada in the Gulf War

United Nations peacekeeping involvements have taken a different turn since the end of the Cold War. The United Nations increasingly enters conflicts where a cease-fire has not yet been arranged, significantly increasing the danger involved for peacekeeping forces.

The Persian Gulf War was the first global crisis in the post-Cold War world. Iraq invaded Kuwait in August 1990. The United Nations passed twelve resolutions to convince Iraq to withdraw its troops. Despite numerous attempts, international **diplomacy** failed, and the conflict escalated to such a level that the United Nations and Iraq could not back down from their positions.

When the Persian Gulf War began, it was like no other war ever fought. The United Nations-sponsored **coalition** force used the most advanced military technology. The air campaign launched against Iraq was the largest in history. Over 100,000 missions were flown, making use of advanced bombing techniques that vastly increased the accuracy of attack. The air operations destroyed most of Iraq's ability to supply its troops and equipment in the field.

IN-DEPTH

Airborne Warning and Control System (AWACS) Aircraft

The airborne warning and control system (AWACS) aircraft is an all-weather surveillance, command, control, and communications centre used by the U.S. military, NATO, and other allied air defence forces.

AWACS has a rotating radar dome that is 9.1 metres in diameter, 1.8 metres thick, and is held 3.33 metres above the fuselage. The radar system enables operators to track objects from Earth's surface up into the stratosphere. The radar can track low-flying aircraft at a range of more than 375.5 kilometres, and it has more range for medium- to high-flying aircraft. The radar has the ability to

eliminate background signals and detect, identify, and track enemy and friendly low-flying aircraft.

Computer consoles display computer-processed data in graphics and tables on video screens. AWACS staff perform jobs that involve surveillance, identification, weapons control, battle management,

■ *Canadian soldiers serve as members of NATO AWACS flight crews.*

and communications. AWACS has a jam-resistant system that continues gathering data while experiencing heavy electronic countermeasures. AWACS can fly for more than 8 hours without refueling.

In March 1977, the first AWACS were delivered to the United States Air Force. AWACS were used in the 1991 Gulf War and proved that they are more than able to coordinate a complex air and ground war. For the first time in aerial warfare, the entire air war fought during the Gulf War was recorded.

Some Canadian troops participated in the Gulf War from the Canadian Forces Base Canada Dry One in Qatar.

FURTHER UNDERSTANDING

Iraqi Invasion of Kuwait

In the 1980s, Iraq owed Kuwait $14 billion. Iraq wanted OPEC to cut oil production, which would cause an increase in oil prices. Higher oil prices would help Iraq repay its debts. Kuwait had a border dispute with Iraq, who accused the Kuwaitis of drilling for oil on Iraqi soil. To give itself more bargaining power in the border dispute, Kuwait increased production, which lowered oil prices. Iraq thought it had done Kuwait and Saudi Arabia a service by fighting Iran, and it wanted its debt to these two countries either renegotiated or cancelled. After failing to resolve their problems through negotiations, Iraq invaded Kuwait in August 1990.

The ground war was a short but intense campaign, resulting in the destruction of Iraq's military machine.

Approximately 4,000 Canadian Forces personnel served in the Gulf War. From the beginning of their deployment in August 1990 to the end of hostilities in April 1991, a maximum of 2,500 personnel were involved at any one time. Approximately 2,000 more troops in Germany and Canada were involved in direct support of the war effort. Canadians sustained no operational casualties during the war.

The United Nations Iraq-Kuwait Observer Mission was established in April 1991. The mission was stationed within a demilitarized zone along the Iraq-Kuwait border. This mission ended in 2003.

Canada also participated in the United Nations Special Commission, which began in April 1991. Its job was to inspect and, if necessary, destroy Iraq's biological, chemical, and nuclear weapons. As well, a small number of Canadian Forces personnel served aboard Airborne Warning and Control System aircraft providing aerial surveillance of the no-fly zones over northern and southern Iraq.

Canada in the Balkans

As the Soviet Empire dissolved in the late 1980s, nationalist feelings swept Eastern Europe, with some nationalist sentiment spilling over into the Balkans.

The Yugoslav Republic was created in 1921 from an assortment of ethnic and cultural groups residing in one area of the Balkan nations. The Balkans had been dominated by other empires for centuries, and as various empires crumbled, they left behind small patches of cultural groups that felt quite isolated from their neighbours.

As the Soviet Empire dissolved in the late 1980s, nationalist feelings swept Eastern Europe, with some nationalist sentiment spilling over into the Balkans. When Slovenia and Croatia declared independence in 1991, and Bosnia-Herzegovina in 1992, the Serbian-dominated Yugoslav army went to war to protect Serbian minorities in these territories.

This civil conflict led to the greatest international refugee crisis since the end of World War II. Including the uprooted people in Croatia, Bosnia-Herzogovina, and elsewhere in the Balkans, the United Nations High Commissioner for refugees estimates there were 1.7 million homeless people in the former Yugoslavia.

Canada's involvement in this crisis has taken several forms. From the beginning of the conflict in September 1991, until August 1994, Canada participated in the European Community Monitor Mission. This non-United Nations mission monitored and reported on the elements of cease-fire agreements and performed other tasks such as humanitarian assistance and confidence-building measures.

In February 1992, the UN created the United Nations Protection Force in Yugoslavia for a 12-month period to create conditions of peace and security. By July 23, 1992, nearly all of the 14,000 military and civilian staff to accomplish this task were in place.

In May 1992, the United Nations imposed an embargo on

■ *In 1993, Canadian peacekeepers went to Kosovo as part of KFOR, the NATO peacekeeping force in Kosovo. They performed many duties, including surveillance with Coyote armoured reconnaissance vehicles.*

Yugoslavian products and commodities, financial and economic contacts, and suspended athletic, scientific, technical, and cultural exchanges. A "no-fly zone" for the Serbian air force was created to stop the Serbian air force from helping the Bosnian Serb ground forces. A small number of Canadian Forces personnel were also assigned to NATO aircraft monitoring the no-fly zone.

Canada was also one of the five nations supporting the airlift of humanitarian supplies into Sarajevo Airport for the United Nations High Commissioner for Refugees. Canada transported more than 10,000 passengers and 21,000 tonnes of relief supplies.

Canada's Major-General Lewis MacKenzie commanded a United Nations peacekeeping force in Bosnia that included about 1,000 Canadians. Replaced by a relief unit in August 1992, the Canadians could do little more than keep the Sarajevo airport open for shipments of humanitarian relief by negotiating several cease-fires.

Canada provided a small number of military personnel for the United Nation's efforts to examine the human rights situation in the former Yugoslavia. The United Nations Commission of Experts was established in 1992 to report on human rights violations. Canada sent a War Crimes Investigation Team to assist this commission in gathering evidence of war crimes in the conflict. Serb forces were accused of a strategy of "ethnic cleansing." Ethnic cleansing is a policy where terror, rape, torture, and looting are used to drive a particular ethnic group from their homes, thus "cleansing" a territory for occupation.

IN-DEPTH

The Yugoslav Wars

The communist state of Yugoslavia was created in 1943. It was divided into six republics—Slovenia, Croatia, Macedonia, Bosnia-Herzegovina, Montenegro, and Serbia—that contain various ethnic groups. It also had two autonomous provinces—Kosovo and Vojvodina. The republics and provinces were ruled by president-for-life Josip Tito. After Tito died in 1980, Slovenia, Croatia, Macedonia, and Bosnia-Herzegovina seceded and formed independent countries.

The Yugoslav wars occurred, in the beginning, to hold the former Yugoslavia together. Except for the short war between Slovenia and Serbia, the Yugoslav wars quickly took on a nationalist character, with Serbia trying to form and sustain Serbian nations in the independent countries of Croatia and Bosnia-Herzegovina.

The first Yugoslav war occurred between Slovenia and Yugoslav (1991). It was mostly bloodless and lasted 10 days.

The second Yugoslav war occurred between Croatia and Serbia (1991–1995). Heavy fighting lasted from 1991 to 1992. In 1992, fighting stopped as the result of a UN-sponsored cease-fire. The war ended in 1995 when Croatia and Serbia signed a peace treaty.

The third Yugoslav war occurred between Bosnia-Herzegovina, Croatia, and Serbia. This war resulted in 278,000 dead and missing people and another 1,325,000 refugees. A 1995 peace treaty divided Bosnia and Herzegovina equally between the Federation of Bosnia and Herzegovina and the Bosnian Serb Republika Srpska.

The Balkans

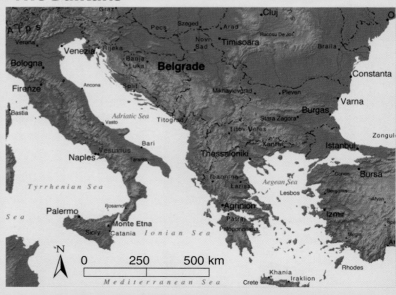

Canada in Africa

Canada has participated in several United Nations operations in Africa. One of the most recent operations was in Somalia, a country of 6 million people. After Somalia won its independence from Britain in 1960, a short-lived democracy was replaced by clan warfare and military domination in 1969.

Somalia became a country without a government. The civil war tore the country apart, with drought and famine making matters even worse.

In November 1991, full-scale war broke out between warring clans. Each clan leader's control of the food supply became a powerful weapon. People who supported the clans got food. Those who did not were left to starve.

While the United Nations was able to broker a cease-fire, it found the scale of human suffering in Somalia almost unimaginable. More than 1 million Somalis were dying. The world responded by sending food aid to halt the massive starvation.

IN-DEPTH

United Nations Peacekeeping Missions

Since 1948, the UN has conducted 56 UN peacekeeping operations. Of these missions, 43 have been created by the United Nations Security Council since 1988. Almost 130 nations have contributed peacekeepers over the years. In 2003, there were active peacekeepers from 89 countries. As of August 31, 2003, there were 15 peacekeeping missions around the world.

Country	Duration
AFRICA	
Western Sahara	April 1991–present
Sierra Leone	Oct. 1999–present
Democratic Republic of the Congo	Nov. 1999–present
Ethiopia and Eritrea	July 2000–present
Côte d'Ivoire	May 2003–present
Liberia	Oct. 2003–present
ASIA	
India/Pakistan	Jan. 1949–present
East Timor	May 2002–present
EUROPE	
Cyprus	Mar 1964–present
Georgia	Aug. 1993–present
Kosovo	June 1999–present
MIDDLE EAST	
Middle East	May 1948–present
Golan Heights	June 1974–present
Lebanon	Mar 1978–present
Iraq/Kuwait	April 1991–present

Cardinal Léger

At the age of 63, Montréal Archbishop Cardinal Léger left Canada for Cameroon, Africa. There he worked to ease the sufferings of people inflicted with leprosy. Léger also set up a centre for people with disabilities in Africa and visited Canada on fund-raising drives for his many projects.

Léger stated, "We have erected a wall of egoism and indifference between us and the people who suffer. Overfed Canadians hide behind their piles of wheat while two-thirds of the world's population are dying of hunger."

Léger also said, "We, in North America, have created a society of abundance and climbed to the summit of civilization. We have all the means to settle our problems—wealth, personnel and energy…Let us help those most in need."

On April 24, 1992, the United Nations Security Council created the United Nations Operations in Somalia to distribute humanitarian aid. On December 3, 1992, this operation was suspended until an enforcement action authorized by the Security Council could ensure the safe delivery of relief. Canada became part of the United Nations coalition force sent to protect the food distribution system.

In May 1993, after the UN decided that their enforcement mission had been successful, the United Nations Operations in Somalia began again. This operation assisted in the provision of humanitarian relief and the economic rehabilitation of Somalia, the repatriation of refugees and displaced persons, the reestablishment of a Somali police force, the development of a program for the removal of mines, and the development of appropriate public information activities.

In 1993, UN peacekeepers arrived in Rwanda to help monitor a cease-fire between the Hutu government and the Tutsi opposition. Canada provided two of the three senior officers in command of the UN force.

When the presidents of Rwanda and Burundi were killed in a plane crash, violence erupted. Soon, UN soldiers were being attacked and killed. Many Western governments withdrew their soldiers from Rwanda, reducing the number of troops from 2,548 to 270.

By 1994, a new government had been established, and the war had ended. More than 500,000 people had died. Four million others had fled the country or were left homeless. Trials against those responsible for violations, such as genocide, began in 1997.

Foreign Aid

Canada is considered part of the developed world.

Canadians often do not realize how fortunate they are. Canada has a reasonably healthy economy and high-quality education and medical programs. Canada has an extensive social program featuring unemployment insurance, workers' compensation, and social assistance.

There are many countries that are not as fortunate. Some people do not have the basics for daily living. More than half the children in the world suffer from lack of food. Some will never see a doctor. Almost half of the world cannot read or write.

The United Nations has divided the world into developed and developing countries. This distinction is based on a country's level of industrial development. Developing countries rely upon traditional farming or fishing techniques and lack the modern industrial infrastructure to compete in the global economy.

Canada is considered part of the **developed world**. The developed world includes the countries in North America, southern and western Europe (except Cyprus, Malta, and Yugoslavia), Australia, Japan, New Zealand, and South Africa.

Some Canadian aid money goes to local literacy programs.

Many developed nations such as Canada feel a sense of responsibility to parts of the world which are not as fortunate. Many developed nations give aid to the **developing world**. Aid can consist of money, education, food, medical supplies, expertise, technology, loans or grants—in short, anything that helps improve the standard of living in poor nations. The United Nations recommends that countries give 0.7 percent of their **Gross National Product** to foreign aid.

Aid is presented in three forms: bilateral, multilateral, and special programs. A bilateral program involves only the party that gives aid and the party which receives it. A large portion of Canada's aid is in this form. This type of aid gives the donor country a great deal of control over the aid package.

Multilateral programs include financial assistance, technical cooperation, humanitarian assistance, and food aid. The assistance is given to an international organization that decides how and where the aid will be used.

Financial assistance is usually passed through international financial institutions such as the World Bank. This assistance involves loans and large-scale investment. Technical cooperation focusses on population, agricultural research, and immunization.

Humanitarian assistance, which is usually managed by UNICEF or the Red Cross, helps the victims of natural catastrophes or war. Food aid is delivered through international organizations, such as the World Food Program or the International Emergency Food Reserve. Special projects are usually handled by a nongovernmental organization (NGO).

IN-DEPTH

Foreign Aid at Work

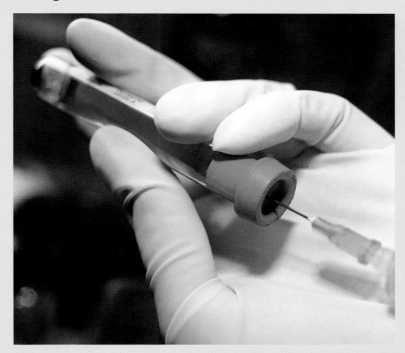

It is estimated that 140 to 250 million children under the age of 5 have a vitamin A deficiency.

In 1992, prompted by a United Nations request for an independent study on a vitamin A supplement, CIDA asked the International Nutrition Program at the University of Toronto to conduct research on the effectiveness of such a supplement.

Vitamin A is essential to human health; deficiency in this vitamin is especially damaging to growing children. Deficiencies can impair growth, bone development, and vision. Severe deficiencies can lead to blindness and death.

The study proved that, by setting up programs of vitamin A supplementation in developing countries, the rate of childhood mortality can be reduced by as much as twenty-three percent. As a result of the study's findings, a 4-day conference on the effectiveness of vitamin A supplementation, attended by fifty-five nutrition specialists—over half of whom came from developing countries—was held in Ottawa in 1993.

The United Nations and other international agencies now use this information when making policies and implementing programs in developing countries. Canada, and in particular the University of Toronto International Nutrition Program, has gained a reputation for excellence in the field of nutrition research.

Benefits of Foreign Aid

CIDA staff provide hope for people in war-torn nations.

Canada began sending aid to other countries shortly after World War II. It was one of the few countries that could afford to provide foreign aid. When the British Empire began dissolving, more countries needing outside aid started to appear. These countries had a combined population of more than 600 million people, most of them poor. They needed help to develop their basic services and farmland. As a member of the Commonwealth, to which many of these countries belonged, Canada felt a special responsibility to assist them.

The Colombo Plan was created in 1950 to assist these Commonwealth countries. The main thrust was toward countries in South Asia. Canada provided $1 billion to the Colombo Plan from 1959 to 1960.

Canada supported other aid projects as well, most of them connected with the United Nations. Canada contributed to the World Health Organization (WHO), which wiped out many dreaded diseases, including smallpox. The Food and Agriculture Organization (FAO) also received money from Canada to purchase fertilizers and promote better farming practices.

Many individuals and nongovernmental organizations also provide assistance. The Unitarian Service Committee, many church groups, and Canadian University Service Overseas (CUSO) have all assisted developing countries. Canadian children collect money for UNICEF, the fund-raising campaign for the United Nations International Children's Emergency Fund. Many retired Canadians volunteer their time to the Canada Executive Services Overseas.

In 1970, the Trudeau Review defined Canada's foreign policy as separate from Great Britain and the United States. The review set several guidelines for providing aid. The review stated that Canada should increase its foreign aid to poorer countries because it was not meeting the amount suggested by the United Nations. Canada's aid should not be limited to solely the United Nations and the Commonwealth. Aid should be presented through a variety of channels. The review also stated that aid should help countries learn to supply their own needs. Previously, aid was provided mainly in crisis situations, such as starvation or disease.

Sometimes aid is given to countries with "strings attached." This means that assistance is given with the requirement that the money be used in a way that will benefit the donor country.

Sometimes recipient countries must use the money to buy the donor country's products. Another common requirement, sometimes unspoken, is that the receiving country remain friendly to the donor country. This is called "tied aid" because the aid is tied to some kind of condition set by the donor.

Although aid is given to improve lives in needy countries, donor nations like Canada also benefit. While tied aid is an obvious example of Canada benefiting directly from foreign aid, some benefits are less direct. For example, many Western countries are giving aid to Russia to help support its new free market economy and preserve its fledgling democratic government. In 1994, Canada agreed to contribute $7 million to Russia. Such aid helps preserve an economy and government in Russia that reflects Canada's own ideals. Some of this $7 million aid package was targeted toward environmental protection for the oil and gas industry, protecting an area of high Canadian investment. Through such aid, Canada helps others while helping itself.

IN-DEPTH

The Benefits of Foreign Aid at a Glance

Canada's foreign aid program contributes to a more just, equitable, and stable world by helping countries that have experienced disaster, conflict, or transition.

Canada's foreign aid program has established Canada's reputation as a committed, constructive member of the international community. This reputation has opened doors and given Canada a stronger voice in world affairs.

Canada has become involved in efforts to resolve global challenges, such as the AIDS pandemic, the ban of land mines, and

environmental problems, such as climate change. Programs to combat these global problems are supported by Canada's foreign aid.

Canada's foreign aid program has been responsible for creating jobs for more than 33,000 Canadians. About 70 cents of every dollar spent on

■ *Canadians are helped economically and socially when assisting people in developing nations.*

foreign aid returns to Canada through the purchase of Canadian goods and services.

Today, more than 2,000 Canadian businesses are gaining entry into growing markets through Canada's foreign aid program.

Each year, around 2,000 Canadian youth work overseas in CIDA-sponsored programs. As a result of these programs, young Canadians are able to broaden their horizons while cultivating their employable skills.

The Role of CIDA

The Canadian International Development Agency (CIDA) was established in 1970. It was created because Canadian agencies responsible for aid distribution often duplicated their efforts. By having one main agency, all Canadian efforts could be coordinated. CIDA's main purpose is to support economic growth and develop social systems in poor countries. Projects are evaluated on the basis of how they can benefit the greatest number of people.

CIDA focussed its attention on Asia, Latin America, and Africa. The countries that needed aid the most received attention first. Recipient nations have many similar problems, while the causes

■ *The availability of clean water is a luxury in many parts of the world. CIDA has completed many water projects throughout the developing world, including one in Peru.*

of problems are sometimes specific to their region.

Africa is usually high on CIDA's priority list. Environmental and economic problems continue to hamper countries on this continent. Nearly every African country receives some assistance from CIDA.

Through CIDA, Canada also assists more than forty countries in Central America, South America, and the Caribbean. These countries suffer from a high population growth rate, unemployment, and rapid urbanization. Rapid urbanization causes problems when cities are overwhelmed by population increases without the services to support them. Some South American countries are relatively developed but are hampered by debt. Small Caribbean states suffer from a lack of natural resources. Many Central American countries are threatened by political terrorists.

In Asia, mass poverty is the biggest problem. CIDA programs in Asia provide basic assistance for the poorest countries and establish commercial and investment links with newly-industrialized countries.

CIDA also promotes links between Canadian educational institutions and their counterparts in developing countries to encourage joint activities. It organizes exchanges between Canadians and people of developing countries. As part of its education initiatives, CIDA co-finances development awareness activities which increase Canadians' awareness of the issues facing developing nations.

CIDA's aid can be found in more than 100 developing countries. The agency assists women's cooperatives in Bangladesh, fights the advance of the desert in the Sahel, participates in a national immunization program in the Philippines, helps a women's credit program in Jamaica, provides a telecommunications network in West Africa, establishes a line of credit in Colombia, and performs countless other activities.

Some CIDA programs work to ease child poverty by funding nutrition, housing, and education initiatives for children in developing nations.

DOCUMENT

Canada's Official Development Assistance Charter (excerpt)

Putting poverty first—the primary purpose of Canadian official development assistance is to help the poorest countries and people of the world.

Helping people to help themselves—Canadian development assistance aims to strengthen the ability of people and institutions in developing countries to solve their own problems in harmony with the natural environment.

Development priorities must prevail—in setting objectives for the aid program. As long as these priorities are met, aid objectives may take into account other foreign policy goals.

Partnership is the key to fostering and strengthening the links between Canada's people and institutions and those of the developing world.

The Future of International Cooperation

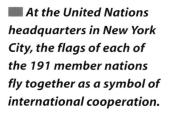

As technological communication and transportation advances place Canadians in increasingly regular contact with the other countries of the world, global cooperation becomes imperative. Technology has made armed conflict increasingly deadly. Nations face the prospect of total destruction if they cannot resolve their differences peacefully.

While organizations such as the United Nations have intervened many times in the last decades to prevent such destruction, their efforts have not been completely successful. Many people want to reform the UN to make it a more effective mediator in global crises. For example, some people think problems exist in the way United Nations leaders are chosen. Some critics suggest that all senior UN positions should be limited to one 7-year term. Many now have unlimited terms. Some UN members argue that the Security Council should be reshaped to reflect global power changes. After World War II, membership on the Security Council was restricted largely to the five major victors.

There are also many problems with the international system of foreign aid. The final goal of aid is, in theory at least, to raise global living standards so that all countries can support their populations.

At the United Nations headquarters in New York City, the flags of each of the 191 member nations fly together as a symbol of international cooperation.

Donor nations sometimes find that their aid is not directed at the best projects to ensure long-term growth and prosperity. There is tension between giving aid to relieve short-term suffering and giving aid to build the infrastructure needed for long-term growth. There is such overwhelming need for short-term relief that sometimes long-term goals are bypassed. Both developed and developing nations fear that some countries will become forever dependent upon international goodwill to survive.

Corruption poses another problem. Occasionally, some leaders or civil servants in developing countries take part of the foreign aid for themselves. In some countries this practice is not considered illegal and is an accepted part of the economy. Attempts to curb this practice by donor nations can result in accusations of cultural interference.

Other critics target donor countries as the source of foreign aid problems. Aid which is given bilaterally is usually given from one government to another. This kind of aid is usually tied aid and is given to more advanced developing countries that can purchase donor countries' products. Between sixty to ninety percent of Canada's foreign aid is bilateral.

Many argue that bilateral aid does not reach the poorest people. They suggest that more aid should be given to multilateral institutions that have less self-interest in determining where aid should be sent. They argue that this aid will be more effective in reaching the very poorest people of the world.

Donor countries argue that they want to keep some control over how their aid is spent or distributed.

Without this control, they fear mismanagement or inefficiency on the part of multilateral groups.

Some people suggest that all international programs are too expensive. Many developed nations face looming economic problems of their own. They argue that countries have a responsibility to take care of their domestic economic and political priorities first.

Others see foreign aid as an issue of human justice. They maintain that developed nations have an inescapable responsibility to help relieve global suffering.

The mechanisms for international cooperation are clearly not perfect. Even the best of intentions can sometimes be misguided or misled. However, it is clear that the future will likely demand more, not less international cooperation. International prosperity, justice, and peace may well depend upon it.

Canadian Expenditures on Foreign Aid

Selected years	% of GNP
1950	.08
1955	.06
1960	.19
1965	.20
1970	.34
1975	.49
1980	.47
1985	.49
1990	.45
1995	.38
2000	.29
2003	.24

Time Line

1914–1918 Canada is recognized as a member of the global community as a result of its participation in World War I.

1931 Canada becomes part of the Commonwealth of Nations.

1939 Canada enters World War II as an independent country.

1945 Canada joins the United Nations.

1949 Canada joins the North Atlantic Treaty Organization (NATO).

1950 Canadian troops are part of the UN force sent to protect South Korea.

1954 Canada begins its long-standing Middle East peacekeeping missions.

1957 Foreign Minister Lester B. Pearson wins the Nobel Peace Prize for his work on the Suez Crisis.

1961 Canadian University Services Overseas (CUSO) is formed.

1964 Canada begins a decades-long peacekeeping mission in Cyprus.

1976 The 1976 Summer Olympics open in Montréal.

1978 The Commonwealth Games are held in Edmonton, Alberta.

1980 Canada announces it will join the boycott of the 1980 Summer Olympics due to the Soviet invasion of Afghanistan.

1981 The Canadarm is first deployed aboard the space shuttle.

Canadian Soldier during World War I

The Commonwealth Games in Edmonton, Alberta, 1976

1986 Canada receives a United Nations award for sheltering refugees.

1989 The Canadian-American Free Trade Agreement comes into effect.

1991 Canadian peacekeepers begin a 5-year mission to El Salvador.

1997 Canada destroys the last land mines in its arsenal.

1998 Canada is elected to a seat on the United Nations Security Council.

2000 The Anik F1, Canada's most powerful communications satellite, is launched.

2002 G8 leaders gather for a summit meeting at Kananaskis, Alberta.

2003 Canada's first space telescope is launched.

Canada's first space telescope

Multiple Choice

Choose the best answer in the multiple choice questions that follow.

1 What piece of Canadian equipment began its service as part of the U.S. space shuttle program in 1981?

a) the Anik F1
b) the RADARSAT 1
c) the Canadarm
d) the Mobile Servicing System

2 Canada considers the Commonwealth of Nations to be what type of tool?

a) a military tool
b) a diplomatic tool
c) an economic tool
d) a political tool

3 Where was the 2002 G8 summit held?

a) Paris, France
b) London, England
c) Rome, Italy
d) Kananaskis, Alberta, Canada

4 Where were the first official Commonwealth Games held?

a) Sydney, Australia
b) Hamilton, Ontario, Canada
c) Cape Town, South Africa
d) London, England

5 How many casualties did Canada suffer during the Korean War?

a) 516
b) 27,000
c) 1,000
d) 1,600

6 When did Canada begin peacekeeping missions in the Middle East?

a) 1954
b) 1949
c) 1961
d) 1990

Mix and Match

Match the description in column A with the correct terms in column B. There are more terms than descriptions.

A	B
1. The Suez Canal is located in this country.	a) Nobel Peace Prize
2. This invasion caused the Gulf War.	b) poverty
3. This person is the symbolic head of the Commonwealth of Nations.	c) 56
4. The UN has conducted this many peacekeeping missions.	d) war
5. This is Asia's largest problem.	e) Iran invaded Iraq
6. Lester B. Pearson won this award.	f) Egypt
	g) Queen Elizabeth II
	h) 43
	i) Iraq's invasion of Kuwait

Time Line

Find the appropriate spot on the time line for each event listed below.

A Canada is elected to a seat on the UN Security Council.

B The Commonwealth Games are held in Edmonton, Alberta.

C The Anik F1, Canada's most powerful communications satellite, is launched.

D Canadian peacekeepers begin a 5-year mission to El Salvador.

E World War I begins.

F G8 leaders meet at Kananaskis, Alberta.

1914 1

1939 World War II begins. Canada enters as an independent country.

1949 Canada joins NATO.

1957 Lester Pearson wins the Nobel Peace Prize for his work on the Suez Canal Crisis.

1961 CUSO is formed.

1964 Canada begins a peacekeeping mission in Cyprus.

1976 The Summer Olympics open in Montréal.

1978 2

1980 Canada announces it will join the boycott of the Summer Olympics due to the Soviet invasion of Afghanistan.

1981 The Canadarm is first deployed aboard the space shuttle.

1986 Canada receives a UN award for sheltering refugees.

1991 3

1997 Canada destroys the last land mine in its arsenal.

1998 4

2000 5

2002 6

2003 Canada's first space telescope is launched.

Further Research

Suggested Reading

Axworthy, Lloyd. *Navigating a New World: Canada's Global Future.* Toronto: Knopf Canada, 2003.

Cook, S. A., R. McLean, and K. O'Rourke. *Framing Our Past: Canadian Women's History in the Twentieth Century.* Montreal: McGill-Queen's University Press, 2001.

Mallory, Enid L. *The Remarkable Years: Canadians Remember the 20th Century.* Markham, ON: Fitzhenry & Whiteside, 2001.

Internet Resources

Canada: A People's History Online
  history.cbc.ca
   The online companion to CBC's award-winning television series on the history of Canada, as told through the eyes of its people. This multimedia Web site features behind-the-scenes information, games, puzzles, and discussion boards.
The site is also available in French.

The Canadian Encyclopedia Online
www.thecanadianencyclopedia.com
A reference for all things Canadian. In-depth history articles are accompanied by photographs, paintings, and maps. All articles can be read in both French and English.

Some Web sites stay current longer than others. To find other Web sites that deal with Canada and its place in the global village, enter terms such as "peacekeeping," "foreign aid," and "United Nations" into a search engine.

Glossary

arms control: a goal of reducing the production and proliferation of weapons

boycott: the refusal to buy goods or services from or associate with another country

coalition: a formal arrangement whereby organizations or countries agree to work together for a specific purpose or period of time

Cold War: a war of words and ideas between the United States and the Soviet Union that stopped short of armed conflict

developed world: the industrialized countries of the world that have fairly high standards of living

developing world: countries of the world which usually have a low level of industrialization, and generally very low standards of living—sometimes called the Third World

diplomacy: the art of conducting and managing relations with other countries

European Community: a bloc of European countries working toward an increasingly integrated economic, monetary, and political union

foreign aid: money given by one country to help another

Gross National Product: the total market value of goods and services produced by a country during a given period

humanitarian aid: aid which improves the welfare of human beings

internationalism: an ideal of international cooperation for the good of all countries

peacekeeping: preventing violence between two or more fighting groups by intervening fairly and impartially

security: safety from danger

trade: the exchange of goods or services for money, goods, or services

treaty: an agreement or arrangement made by negotiation between two or more groups

Answers

Multiple Choice	Mix and Match	Time Line
1. c)	1. f)	1. e)
2. b)	2. i)	2. b)
3. d)	3. g)	3. d)
4. b)	4. c)	4. a)
5. d)	5. b)	5. c)
6. a)	6. a)	6. f)

Index